CONTENTS

Beginner

PAGE 15

Easy

MW00851314

Intermediate

PAGE 36

Experienced

PAGE 18

SPARKLE Wrap

YOU'LL NEED:

YARN
3½oz/100g or 160yd/150m of any beaded or sequined worsted weight yarn

NEEDLES
One size 15 (10mm) circular needle, 29"/74cm long *or size to obtain gauge*

ADDITIONAL MATERIALS
Stitch marker

FINISHED MEASUREMENTS
Approx 12½ x 51½ "/31.5 x 130.5cm.

GAUGE
8 sts and 16 rows = 4"/10cm over pat st using size 15 (10mm) needles.
Take time to check gauge.

STITCH GLOSSARY
Inc 2 Knit into the front, back and front of same stitch.

WRAP
Cast on 3 sts. Knit one row on WS.
Row 1 (RS) Inc 2, k to end—5 sts. Mark as RS.
Rows 2–9 Inc 2, k to end—21 sts.
Row 10 (WS) Inc 2, p to end—23 sts.
Rows 11–17 Inc 2, k to end—37 sts.
Row 18 (WS) Rep row 10—39 sts.
Rep rows 11–18 four times more—103 sts.
Bind off.

Rose Callahan

SELF STRIPING Shawl

Jack Deutsch

YOU'LL NEED:

YARN (5)
10½oz/300g or 610yd/540m of any bulky weight variegated wool blend

NEEDLES
Size 10½ (6.5mm) circular needle, 29" (73.5cm) long *or size to obtain gauge*

FINISHED MEASUREMENTS
Length from neck to point Approx 18"/45.5cm.
Length from point to each front edge Approx 40"/101.5cm.

GAUGE
13 sts and 16 rows = 4"/10cm over St st using size 10½ (6.5mm) needle
Take time to check gauge.

STITCH GLOSSARY
SEED STITCH
Row 1 (RS) *K1, p1; rep from * to end.
Row 2 K the purl and p the knit sts.
Rep row 2 for seed st.

NOTE
Shawl is worked back and forth in rows on circular needle.

SHAWL
Cast on 130 sts. Working back and forth, work in seed st for 4 rows.
Next row (RS) Work 4 sts in seed st, work in St st to last 4 sts, work in seed st to end. Cont in pat as established until piece measures 17"/43cm from beg, end on a WS row.

SHAPE SHAWL AT LEFT NECK EDGE
Next row (RS) Work 74 sts in seed st, work 52 sts in St st, work in seed st to end. **Next row** Work 4 sts in seed st, work 52 sts in St st, work in seed st to end. Rep last 2 rows once more.
Next row (RS) Bind off 70 sts in seed st, work 4 sts in seed st, work 52 sts in St st, work in seed st to end—60 sts. Cont in pat as established, working left front piece of shawl until piece measures 39"/99cm from cast-on edge. Work in seed st for 4 rows. Bind off all sts in pat.

FINISHING
Block piece to measurements.

ENTRELAC Wrap

YOU'LL NEED:

YARN (4)
7oz/200g or 660yd/610m of any worsted weight wool in green (A) and purple (B)

NEEDLES
One pair size 9 (5.5mm) needles *or size to obtain gauge*

ADDITIONAL MATERIALS
Size 9 (5.5mm) circular needle, 16"/40cm long

FINISHED MEASUREMENTS
Approx 19" x 72"/48cm x 183cm.

GAUGES
16 sts and 24 rows = 4"/10cm over St st and 11 sts = 4"/10cm over entrelac pat using size 9 (5mm) needles.
Take time to check gauges.

STITCH GLOSSARY
SEED ST
Row 1 (RS) *K1, p1; rep from * end, k1.
Row 2 K the purl sts and p the knit sts.
Rep row 2 for seed st.

SLIP ST PAT
Row 1 (RS) With A, k 3, sl 1, *k2, sl 1; rep from * to last st, k1. **Row 2** P1, *sl 1, p 2; rep from * to last st, p1. **Row 3** Change to B, k 1, *sl 1, k 2; rep from * to last st, k 1. **Row 4** P3, sl 1, *p 2, sl 1; rep from * to last st, p1. **Row 5** Change to A, k 2, *sl 1, k 2; rep from * to end. **Row 6** P2, *sl 1, p 2; rep from * to end. **Rows 7 and 8** With B, rep rows 1 and 2. **Rows 9 and 10** With A, rep rows 3 and 4. **Rows 11 and 12** With B, rep rows 5 and 6.

WRAP
With A, cast on 83 sts. Work 1 row in seed st. Change to B and work 2 rows garter st (k every row).
Next row (RS) Change to A work 12 rows sl st pat. K 2 rows.
Next row (RS) Change to B, k1, *k2tog; rep from * to end—42 sts.

BEG ENTRELAC PAT
Base triangles–*Next row (WS)
With B, p 2, turn; k 2, turn; p 3, turn; k 3, turn; p4, turn; k 4; cont in this way, working 1 more p st every other row until there are 6 p sts (1 triangle complete). Rep from * to end.

First row of rectangles
Beg edge triangle–Next row (RS) With A, k2, turn; k 1, p 1, turn; inc in first st, ssk, turn; k 1, p 1, turn; inc in first st, p1, put yarn in back, ssk, turn; [k 1, p 1] twice, k 1, turn; inc in first st, p 1, k 1, p 1, put yarn in back, ssk (edge triangle complete).

Rectangles
*Pick up and k 6 sts evenly along edge of next triangle, turn; beg with k 1, work 6 sts in seed st, turn; beg with p 1, work 5 sts in seed st, ssk; rep last 2 steps 6 times (1 rectangle completed). Rep from * to * across row, to edge of last triangle.

Ending edge triangle
Pick up and k 6 sts evenly along edge of this triangle, turn; p2tog, work 4 sts in seed st, turn; work 5 sts in seed st, turn; k2tog, work 3 sts in seed st, turn; work 4 sts in seed st, turn; p2tog, work 2 sts in seed st, turn; work 3 sts in seed st, turn; k2tog, p 1, turn; k 1, p 1, turn; p2tog, leave rem st on RH needle, cut yarn.

Second row of rectangles
With B, cont from st on RH needle, pick up and p 5 sts evenly along edge of triangle just worked. [Turn; k 6, turn; p 5, p2tog] 6 times. *Pick up and p 6 sts evenly along side of next rectangle, [turn; k 6, turn; p 5, p2tog] 6 times; rep from * to end. Cut yarn.

Third row of rectangles
With A, work as for base triangles, but pick up sts along side edge of rectangles instead of triangles.
Cont to work in entrelac pat until work measures 64"/162.5cm from beg.

Final row of triangles
With B, cont from st on RH needle, pick up and p 5 sts evenly along edge of triangle just worked, turn; k 6, turn; p 5, p2tog, turn; k 5, turn; p 4, p2tog, turn; k 4, turn; p 3, p2tog, turn; k 3, turn; p 2, p2tog, turn; k2, turn; p1, p2tog, turn; k1, turn; p2tog. Rep from * to end, picking up sts from side of rectangles instead of triangles.

Slip st borders
Change to A, k1, inc 1 st in every st to end—83 sts. K 1 row. Change to B, beg with row 3 of sl st pat and work rows 3-12, then rows 1 and 2. K 2 rows. Change to A, k 1 row. Bind off.

Slip st edges (work along each long edge)
With RS facing, with A and circular needle, pick up and k 368 sts. K 1 row. Change to B, beg with row 3 of Sl st pat and work rows 3-12, then rows 1 and 2. K 2 rows. Change to A, k 1 row. Bind off.

Border edge triangles
(Work along each short edge after sl st borders have been worked.) With RS facing, A, and circular needle, pick up and k 96 sts. K 1 row.
Next row K2, *turn; k 1, p 1, turn (cont in seed st throughout); work 3, turn; work 3, turn; work 4, turn, work 4, turn; work 5, turn, work 5, turn; cont in this way until 12 sts on both rows have been worked. Bind off 12*. With 1 st left on RH needle, change to B, k1. Rep from * to *. Work 6 more triangles along edge in this way, alternating colors for each triangle.

FINISHING
Make pom-poms. Sew in ends. Block. Sew on pom-poms.

FRINGED Triangle Shawl

Jack Deutsch

FINISHED MEASUREMENTS
Length from neck to point 32"/81cm.
Circumference around lower edge 60"/152cm.

GAUGE
14 sts and 24 rows = 4"/10cm over garter st using smaller needles and MC.
Take time to check gauge.

STITCH GLOSSARY
SEMICIRCLE CENTER
Rows 1 (WS), 4, 7, 10, 13, and 16 *K1, [yo] twice; rep from * to last st, k1.
Row 2 (RS), 5, 8, 11, 14, and 17 K, dropping all yo's.
Rows 3 and 9 Knit.

YOU'LL NEED:

YARN (4)
12¼oz/350g or 840yd/780m of any worsted weight nylon blend in light blue (MC)
3½oz/100g or 240yd/220m of any worsted weight ribbon yarn in blue multi (A)

NEEDLES
One pair each sizes 10 and 15 (6 and 10mm) needles *or size to obtain gauge*

ADDITIONAL MATERIALS
Size H/8 (5mm) crochet hook

Row 6 [K1, k2tog] 18 times—36 sts.
Row 12 [K1, k2tog] 12 times—24 sts.
Row 15 [K1, k2tog] 8 times—18 sts.
Row 18 K2tog across—9 sts.

SHAWL
With smaller needles and MC, cast on 5 sts.
Row 1 (RS) K2, yo, k to last 2 sts, yo, k2—7 sts.
Row 2 Knit. Rep last 2 rows 65 times more—137 sts.
Shape semicircle neck opening as follows:
Next row (RS) K2, yo, work 52 sts, join a 2nd ball of yarn and bind off center 29 sts, work to last 2 sts, yo, k2. Working both sides at once, cont side edge inc's every RS row, bind off from each neck edge 4 sts once, 3 sts 3 times, 2 sts 3 times.
Next (dec) row (RS) Cont incs as established and work to last 3 sts of first side, ssk, k1; on 2nd side, k1, k2tog, work to end. Rep dec row every other row twice, every 4th row 4 times, every 6th row twice. Work even at semicircle neck opening and cont to inc at side edges until there are 60 sts on each side of neck edge, end on a RS row. Bind off 60 sts each side.
Semicircle center
With MC, work 1 row of sc around semicircle neck opening. With larger needles and A, pick up and k 54 sts around the sc. Work 18 rows of semicircle center. Break yarn and weave through rem loops. Pull up and secure.

FINISHING
Block piece to measurements.

FRINGE
With A, cut 11"/28cm lengths and attach 2 strands each in every other hole of lower edge.

DIAMOND Shawl

Jack Deutsch

YOU'LL NEED:

YARN ❹
7oz/200g or 370yd/340m of any worsted weight variegated wool

NEEDLES
One pair each sizes 8 and 10 (5 and 6mm) needles *or size to obtain gauge*

FINISHED MEASUREMENTS
Length from neck to point
Approx 16"/40.5cm.
Circumference around lower edge
Approx 56"/142cm.

GAUGE
12 sts and 24 rows = 4"/10cm over garter st using smaller needles.
Take time to check gauge.

NOTE
Shawl is worked from top down.

SHAWL
With larger needles, cast on 130 sts. Change to smaller needles. Work double eyelet rows as foll:
Rows 1 and 2 Knit.
Row 3 K1, *k2tog, yo; rep from * to last 3 sts, k3.
Rows 4–6 K1, k2tog, yo, k2tog, k to end—127 sts.
Row 7 K1, k2tog, *yo, k2tog; rep from * to last 3 sts, k3—126 sts.
Row 8 K1, k2tog, yo, k1, k2tog, yo, k2tog, k to end—125 sts.
Rep row 8 ten times more—115 sts.

BEG CHART
Cont working edge sts every row as established in row 8 of double eyelet rows, AT THE SAME TIME, work in chart as foll:
Note Only odd (RS) rows are shown on chart. K every even (WS) row.
Row 1 Work 44 sts, beg with row 1,

work 27 sts of chart, k to end. Cont in pat as established, working 90 rows of chart and working every WS (even) row as k across all sts—25 sts when chart complete. Work even, cont to work edge sts until 14 sts rem.

MAKE POINT
Row 1 K1, k2tog, yo, k1, k2tog, yo, SK2P, yo, k5—13 sts.
Row 2 K1, k2tog, yo, k1, k2tog, yo, SSK, k4—12 sts.
Row 3 K1, k2tog, yo, k2tog, k to end 11—sts.
Rep row 3 six times more—5 sts.
Next row Knit.
Next row K1, k2tog, k2—4 sts.
Next row K1, k2tog, k1—3 sts.
Next row SK2P, fasten off last st.

FINISHING
Block piece to measurements.

TASSELS (make 3)
Cut 20 12"/30.5cm strands of yarn. Fold in half and tie 1 strand through middle to tie to point of shawl and 1 strand around tassel approx 2"/5cm from top (see photo). Tie one tassel to each point of shawl.

Stitch Key

⊙ Yarn over

◩ Knit 2 together

◪ SSK

⋏ SK2P

☐ Knit

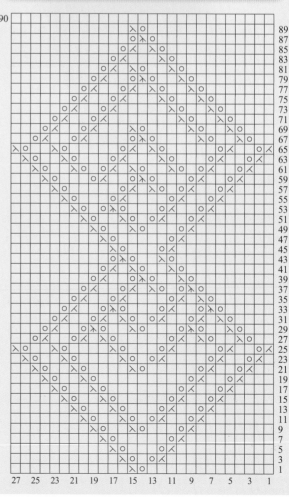

REVERSIBLE CABLE Shawl

Jack Deutsch

FINISHED MEASUREMENTS
Approx 17 x 64"/43 x 162.5cm.

GAUGE
21 sts and 20 rows = 4"/10cm over st pat using larger needles.
Take time to check gauge.

STITCH GLOSSARY
8-st RC Sl 4 sts to cn and hold to *back*, [p1, k1] twice, [p1, k1] twice from cn.
8-st LC Sl 4 sts to cn and hold to *front*, [p1, k1] twice, [p1, k1] twice from cn.

STITCH PATTERN
(multiple of 12 sts plus 6)
Row 1 (RS) Sl 1, k2, *8-st RC, [p1, k1] twice; rep from * to last 3 sts, end k3.
Rows 2–6 Sl 1, k2, *p1, k1; rep from * to last 3 sts, end k3.
Row 7 (RS) Sl 1, k2, *[p1, k1] twice, 8-st LC; rep from * to last 3 sts, end k3.
Rows 8–12 Sl 1, k2, *p1, k1; rep from * to last 3 sts, end k3.
Repeat rows 1–12 for st pat.

SHAWL
With smaller needles, cast on 90 sts.
Next row Sl 1 purlwise, k2, *p1, k1; rep from * to last 3 sts, end k3.
Rep last row until piece measures 1"/2.5cm from beg. Change to larger needles.
Work in pat st until piece measures 63"/160cm, end with row 1 or row 7. Change to smaller needles.
Next row (WS) Sl 1 purlwise, k2, *p1, k1; rep from * to last 3 sts, end k3.
Rep last row until piece measures 64"/162.5cm from beg. Bind off firmly.

FINISHING
Block piece to measurements.

7

LACY ZIGZAG Shawl

YOU'LL NEED:

YARN 1
6¼oz/175g or 1200yd/1100m of any fingering weight wool

NEEDLES
One pair size 5 (3.75mm) needles *or size to obtain gauge*
Size 5 (3.75mm) circular needle, 24"/60cm long

ADDITIONAL MATERIALS
Size D/3 (3.25mm) crochet hook
Contrasting sport weight yarn (waste yarn)
Stitch markers (one a different color)

FINISHED MEASUREMENTS
Approx 22"/56cm wide x 66"/167.5cm long.

GAUGES
21sts and 32¼ rows = 4"/10cm over chart 1 after blocking and
19 sts and 20 rows = 4"/10cm over border pat rib after blocking using size 5 (3.75mm) needles.
Take time to check gauges.

STITCH GLOSSARY
pm place marker
lp(s) loops

Jack Deutsch

Chart 1

30-st rep

SHAWL

With crochet hook and waste yarn, ch 102. Cut yarn and draw end though lp on hook. Turn ch so bottom lps are at top and cut end is at LH side. With straight needles, beg 2 lps from opposite end, pick up and k 1 st in each of next 95 lps. Purl one row.

BEG CHART 1

Row 1 (RS) Beg with st 1 and work through st 47, rep sts 18–47 once, then work sts 48 to 65. Cont to foll chart in this manner through row 20, then rep rows 1–20 for 24 times more. Place sts on a length of waste yarn.

FINISHING

Block piece to measurements.

BORDER

Place sts from waste yarn on LH needle ready for a RS row.
Prep rnd With circular needle, knit, dec 9 sts evenly spaced across sts on needle, (pm, yo, pm) for 1st corner, pick up and k 247 sts along side edge, (pm, yo, pm) for 2nd corner, with RS facing, release cut end from lp of waste yarn ch at beg edge, pull out 1 ch at a time, placing sts on LH needle, then knit dec 9 sts evenly spaced across sts on needle, (pm, yo, pm) for 3rd corner, pick up and k 247 sts along side, (pm, yo, pm of different color to indicate beg of rnd) for last corner—670 sts.
Next rnd Purl.
Rnd 1 [*P2, yo, ssk, k1, k2tog, yo; rep from * to 2 sts before marker, p2, sl marker, work row 3 of chart 2, sl marker] 4 times.
Rnd 2 [*P2, k5; rep from * to 2 sts before marker, p2, sl marker, work row 4 of chart 2, sl marker] 4 times.
Rnd 3 [*P2, k1, yo, SK2P, yo, k1; rep from * to 2 sts before marker, p2, sl marker, work row 5 of chart 2, sl marker] 4 times.

Rnd 4 [*P2, k5; rep from * to 2 sts before marker, p2, sl marker, work row 6 of chart 2, sl marker] 4 times.
Rnd 5 Rep rnd 1, working row 7 of chart 2 between markers at corners.
Rnd 6 Rep rnd 2, working row 8 of chart 2 between markers at corners.
Rnd 7 Rep rnd 3, working row 9 of chart 2 between markers at corners
Rnd 8 Rep rnd 4, working row 10 of chart 2 between markers at corners.
Rep rnds 1–4 twice more, then rnds 1–3 once, AT THE SAME TIME, cont to work chart 2 rows 11–21 as established.
Bind off as foll: with WS facing and crochet hook, [insert hook into next st on needle, yo and draw up a lp, slip st off needle and onto hook] twice, yo and draw through 2 lps on hook,*insert hook into next st on needle, yo and draw up a lp, slip st off needle and onto hook, yo and draw through 2 lps on hook; rep from * to end. Cut yarn, fasten off last st.

Chart 2

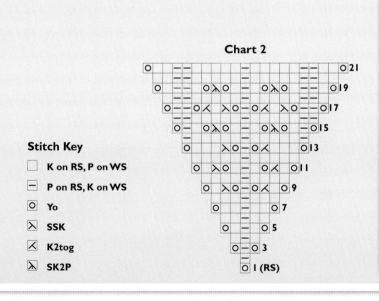

Stitch Key

- ☐ K on RS, P on WS
- — P on RS, K on WS
- ○ Yo
- ⟍ SSK
- ⟋ K2tog
- ⅄ SK2P

RIBBON Wrap

YOU'LL NEED

YARN 4 5
1¾oz/50g or 460yd/420m of any worsted weight mohair blend in olive (A)
3½oz/100g or 120yd/110m of any bulky weight variegated ribbon yarn in blue/green (B)

NEEDLES
One each sizes 8 and 10½ (5 and 6.5mm) circular needles, 24"/60cm long *or size to obtain gauge*

ADDITIONAL MATERIALS
Size F/5 (3.75mm) crochet hook

FINISHED MEASUREMENTS
Approx 42 x 42"/106.5 x 106.5cm.

GAUGE
12 sts and 20 rows = 4"/10cm over rev St st using larger needles.
Take time to check gauge.

NOTE
Shawl is worked back and forth in rows on circular needles. *Do not* join to work circularly.

SHAWL
With larger needle and B, cast on 120 sts. K 1 row.

BEG STRIPE PAT
Next row (RS) With A, work in rev St st (p on RS, k on WS) for 10 rows.
Next row (RS) Do not cut A, tie on B, leaving a 12"/30.5cm tail. Work 1 row even in B only.
Cut B, leaving a 12"/30.5cm tail. Push sts back to opposite end of needle and pick up A.
Rep last 11 rows for stripe pat 6 times more. Work 5 rows A once more.

SHAPE NECK
Next row Bind off 80 sts. Change to smaller needles and complete stripe pat on rem 40 sts.

Work 11-row stripe pat 3 times more. Change to larger needles. Work 4 rows stripe pat, cast on 80 sts. Complete stripe pat on 120 sts. Work 11-row stripe pat 6 times more. Bind off in B.

FINISHING
With crochet hook and B, work one row sc around inside of neck edge. Using photo as guide, use crochet hook to pull up loops, as desired, along rows of B in all stripe pat sections. Secure the long tails around edge by tying A and B together.

Jack Deutsch

COLORBLOCK Wrap

YOU'LL NEED:

YARN
5¼oz/150g or 330yd/300m of any worsted weight wool blend in dark brown (A), green (B), pink (C), and orange (D)

NEEDLES
One pair size 8 (5mm) needles, *or size to obtain gauge*

ADDITIONAL MATERIALS
Size H/8 (5mm) crochet hook and stitch markers

FINISHED MEASUREMENTS
Approx 24 x 64"/61 x 162.5cm.

GAUGE
18 sts and 28 row = 4"/10cm over St st

using size 8 (5mm) needles.
Take time to check gauge.

STITCH GLOSSARY
SEED STITCH
(over an even number of sts)
Row 1 *K1, p1; rep from *.
Row 2 *P1, k1; rep from *. Rep rows 1 and 2 for seed st.

NOTE
When changing colors, twist yarns on WS to prevent holes in work.

WRAP
With A, cast on 28 sts; with B, cast on 28 sts; with C, cast on 28 sts; with D, cast on 28 sts—112 sts. **Next row (RS)** Work in Seed st over first 6 sts, place marker (pm), work in St st and color block pat as established to last 6 sts, pm, work in seed st to end.

Jenny Acheson

Maintaining first and last 6 sts in seed st for side borders, and color block pat as established, work until piece measures 64"/162.5cm from beg, ending with a WS row. Bind off in color block pat.

FRINGE
Cut 48 strands in each color approx 20"/51cm long. Fold in half and with crochet hook, pull loop though st at edge. Place 4 fringes of 6 strands in each color evenly across cast-on and bound-off edges. Trim neatly.

SOFT and Simple

Jack Deutsch

FINISHED MEASUREMENTS
Length from neck to point Approx 29"/73.5cm.
Circumference around upper edge Approx 46½"/118cm.

GAUGE
18 sts and 28 rows = 4"/10cm over St st using size 8 (5mm) needles.
Take time to check gauge.

SHAWL
BEG LOWER POINT
Cast on 3 sts.
Row 1 (RS) [K1, yo] twice, k1—5 sts.
Row 2 and all WS rows Purl.
Row 3 K2, yo, k1, yo, k2—7 sts.
Row 5 K3, yo, k1, yo, k3—9 sts.
Row 7 K4, yo, work in St st to last 4 sts, yo, k4—11 sts.

YOU'LL NEED:

YARN
7oz/200g or 600yd/560m of any worsted weight merino wool blend

NEEDLES
One pair size 8 (5mm) needles *or size to obtain gauge*

Row 8 K4, work in St st to last 4 sts, k4. Rep rows 7 and 8, working first and last 4 sts in garter st (k every row), until 209 sts are on needle. Work 4 rows in garter st. Bind off.

FINISHING
Block piece to measurements.

PAINTER'S Palette

YOU'LL NEED:

YARN (4)
15¾oz/450g or 1100yd/900m of any worsted weight self-striping wool blend

NEEDLES
Size 7 (4.5mm) circular needle, 24"/60cm long *or size to obtain gauge*

ADDITIONAL MATERIALS
Size 7 (4.5mm) crochet hook
Cable needle
Stitch holders

Jack Deutsch

CABLE PATTERN
Row 1 Sl 1, k to center 4 sts, yo, RC, yo, k to end.
Rows 2 and 4 Sl 1, k to cable, p4, k to end.
Row 3 Sl 1, k to 1 st before cable, p1, k4, p1, k to end.
Rep rows 1–4 for cable pat.

SHAWL PANEL (make 5)
Cast on 1 st.
Row 1 Inc 1—2 sts.
Rows 2, 4, 6, 8, and 10 Purl.
Row 3 Inc in both sts across—4 sts.
Rows 5 and 9 Knit.
Row 7 K1, yo, k2, yo, k1—6 sts.
Row 11 Sl 1, yo, RC, yo, k1—8 sts.
Rows 12 and 14 Sl 1 purlwise, k1, p4, k2.
Row 13 Sl 1, p1, k4, p1, k1.
Row 15 Sl 1, k1, yo, RC, yo, k2—10 sts.
Rows 16 and 18 Sl 1, k2, p4, k3.
Row 17 Sl 1, k1, p1, k4, p1, k2.
Row 19 Work Row 1 of cable pat—12 sts.
Rows 20–42 Work rows 2–4 of cable pat, then rep rows 1–4 five times more—22 sts.
Row 43 (eyelet row) Sl 1, [yo, k2tog] to cable, yo, RC, [yo, ssk] to last st, yo, k1—24 sts.
Rows 44–74 Work rows 2–4 of cable pat, then rep rows 1–4 seven times more—38 sts.
Row 75 (eyelet row) Same as row 43—40 sts.
Rows 76–114 Work rows 2–4 of cable pat, then rep rows 1–4 nine times more—58 sts.
Row 115 (eyelet row) Same as row 43—60 sts.
Rows 116–160 Work rows 2–4 of cable pat, then rep rows 1–4 six times more, rep rows 1 and 2 once more—82 sts.
Place all sts on holder.

▉▉▉▊▭

FINISHED MEASUREMENTS
Length from neck to point
Approx 25"/63.5cm.
Circumference around lower edge
Approx 50"/127cm.

GAUGE
16 sts and 30 rows = 4"/10cm over garter st using size 7 (4.5mm) needle.
Take time to check gauge.

STITCH GLOSSARY
RC (right cable) Sl 2 sts to cn and hold to *back*, k2, k2 from cn.

MB (make bobble) With 1 st on RH needle;
Row 1 Yo, k1, turn.
Rows 2 and 4 K across, turn.
Row 3 [K1, yo] twice, k1, turn.
Rows 5–12 K across, turn.
Row 13 K1, SK2P, k1.
Row 14 K across, turn.
Row 15 SK2P.
Fold bobble in half, sl final st under back of yo st from row 1.

FINISHING

Arrange panels side by side. With WS together and crochet hook, sl st panels together, working just inside selvage sl st.

BORDER

With sts on holders, begin working tops of panels as foll:
Row 1 Sl 1 purlwise, *k80 sts from first panel, k2tog (1 st each from 1st and 2nd panels); rep from * across all panels, end k81—406 sts.
Rows 2, 4, 5, 6, and 8 Sl 1, k across.
Row 3 Sl 1, k39, *M1, k2, M1, k79; rep from * 3 times, k40.
Row 7 Sl 1, k40, *M1, k2, M1, k81; rep from * 3 times, k41.
Row 9 Bind off 42 sts, *MB, bind off 84 sts; rep from * 3 times. MB, bind off rem sts, leaving last st on needle.

FRONT EDGE

Working across ends of panels, pick up sts as foll:
Row 1 Pick up and k 80 sts across side of 1st panel, 1 st from center of each panel (where panels meet at top), 80 sts across side of last panel.
Rows 2–8 Sl 1, k across.
Bind off all sts.

YOU'LL NEED:

YARN (3)
8¾oz/250g or 580yd/530m of any DK weight cotton

NEEDLES
One pair size 9 (5.5mm) needles *or size to obtain gauge*

FINISHED MEASUREMENTS
Approx 21½ x 55"/54.5cm x 139.5cm

GAUGE
14 sts and 18 rows = 4"/10cm over st pat using size 9 (5.5mm) needles. *Take time to check gauge.*

STITCH GLOSSARY
STITCH PATTERN
(multiple of 11 sts plus 1)
Row 1 and all WS rows Purl.
Row 2 K1, *k2tog, k4, [yo, k1] twice, ssk, k1; rep from * to end.
Row 4 K1, *k2tog, k3, yo, k1, yo, k2, ssk, k1; rep from * to end.
Row 6 K1, *k2tog, k2, yo, k1, yo, k3, ssk, k1; rep from * to end.
Row 8 K1, *k2tog, [k1, yo] twice, k4, ssk, k1; rep from * to end.

Row 10 K1, *k2tog, yo, k1, yo, k5, ssk, k1; rep from * to end.
Row 12 Rep row 8.
Row 14 Rep row 6.
Row 16 Rep row 4.
Row 18 Rep row 2.
Row 20 K1, *k2tog, k5, yo, k1, yo, ssk, k1; rep from * to end.
Rep rows 1–20 for st pat.

WRAP
Cast on 75 sts. Work 4 rows in garter st.

BEG ST PAT
Row 1 (WS) K4, work row 1 of st pat, k4.
Cont in pat as established, working rows 1–20 and keeping first and last 4 sts each side in garter st (k every row) until piece measures 54"/137cm. Work 4 rows in garter st. Bind off.

FINISHING
Block pieces to measurements.

Jack Deutsch

SCALLOP EDGE Wrap

YOU'LL NEED:

YARN 4 5

8¼oz/250g or 620yd/565m of any variegated worsted weight wool blend (A)

3½oz/100g or 140yd/100m of any bulky weight ribbon yarn in orange (B)

NEEDLES

One pair size 10 (6mm) needles *or size to obtain gauge*

FINISHED MEASUREMENTS

Approx 43½ x 12½"/110.5 x 32cm.

GAUGE

15 sts and 22 rows = 4"/10cm over St st using size 10 (6mm) needles and 2 strands of A held together.
Take time to check gauge.

NOTES

1 Use 2 strands of A held together throughout.
2 When joining B, leave approx 6"/15cm tail at each end for decoration at lower edge of shawl.

SHAWL

With 2 strands of B held together, cast on 44 sts. Work 2 rows in garter st. Change to 2 strands A held together and work in st pat as foll:
BEG ST PAT
Row 1 (RS) With 2 strands of A held together, knit.
Row 2 K10, p20, k2, yo, k2tog, k5, yo, k2tog, yo, k3—45 sts.
Row 3 K1, yo, k2tog, k to end.
Row 4 K10, p20, k2, yo, k2tog, k4, yo, [k2tog, yo] twice, k3—46 sts.
Row 5 Rep row 3.
Row 6 K10, p20, k2, yo, k2tog, k3, yo, [k2tog, yo] 3 times, k3—47 sts.
Row 7 Rep row 3.
Row 8 K10, p20, k2, yo, k2tog, k2, yo, [k2tog, yo] 4 times, k3—48 sts.

Row 9 Rep row 3.
Row 10 K10, p20, k2, yo, k2tog, k1, yo, [k2tog, yo] 5 times, k3—49 sts.
Row 11 Rep row 3.
Row 12 K10, p20, k2, yo, k2tog, k1 [k2tog, yo] 5 times, k2tog, k2—48 sts.
Row 13 Rep row 3.
Row 14 K10, p20, k2, yo, k2tog, k2, [k2tog, yo] 4 times, k2tog, k2—47 sts.
Row 15 Rep row 3.
Row 16 K10, p20, k2, yo, k2tog, k3, [k2tog, yo] 3 times, k2tog, k2—46 sts.
Row 17 Rep row 3.
Row 18 K10, p20, k2, yo, k2tog, k4, [k2tog, yo] twice, k2tog, k2—45 sts.
Row 19 Rep row 3.
Row 20 K10, p20, k2, yo, k2tog, k5, k2tog, yo, k2tog, k2—44 sts.
Row 21 Change to single strand of B. Knit.
Row 22 Knit.
Rep the last 22 rows 10 times more. With B, k 1 row. Bind off knitwise with B.

SHOULDER EDGING

With RS facing and 2 strands of B held tog, pick up and k 125 sts along top edge of shawl.
Next row (WS) Knit.
Next (dec) row (RS) K12, [k2tog, k9] 9 times, k2tog, k12—115 sts. Bind off knitwise.

FINISHING

Block piece to measurements.

SHOULDER TIES

Cut two 40"/101.5cm lengths of B, fold in half and attach folded loops at front edges.
Finish all ends of B at lower edge by securing with a knot at base of shawl. Trim ends at a slanted angle to prevent fraying.

Jack Deutsch

POCKET Shawl

YOU'LL NEED:

YARN
24½oz/700g or 770yd/700m of any super bulky variegated acrylic

NEEDLES
One pair each sizes 10 and 10½ (6 and 6.5mm) needles *or size to obtain gauge*

FINISHED MEASUREMENTS
Approx 11½ x 65"/29 x 165cm.

GAUGE
20 sts and 20 rows = 4"/10cm over rib pat using larger needles.
Take time to check gauge.

STITCH GLOSSARY
RIB PATTERN
Row 1 (RS) K4, *p1, k3; rep from * to last 2 sts, p1, k1.
Row 2 *K3, p1; rep from * to last 2 sts, k2.
Rep these 2 rows for rib pat.

SHAWL
With larger needles, cast on 58 sts. Work in rib pat until piece measures 65"/165cm, end with a RS row. Bind off in rib pat on WS.

POCKET 1
With larger needles, cast on 34 sts. Work in rib pat until piece measures 7"/18cm, end with a WS row. Change to smaller needles.
Next row (RS) *K2, p2tog; rep from * to last 2 sts, k2—26 sts. Work in garter st for 1"/2.5cm, end with a WS row. Bind off.

POCKET 2
With smaller needles, cast on 26 sts. Work in garter st for 1"/2.5cm, end with a WS row. Change to larger needles.
Next row (RS) K2, inc 1 st in next k st, *p1, k1, inc 1 st in next k st; rep from * to end—34 sts. Work in rib pat until piece measures same as pocket 1. Bind off in rib.

FINISHING
Center and sew pocket 1 2½"/6.5cm from cast-on edge, making sure to match rib pat. Center and sew pocket 2 2½"/6.5cm from bound off edge, being sure to match rib pat.

Jack Deutsch

TEXTURED Shawl

Jack Deutsch

FINISHED MEASUREMENTS
Approx 27"/68.5cm wide x 72"/183cm long excluding fringe.

GAUGE
20 sts and 27½ rows = 4"/10cm over pat st using size 8 (5mm) needles.
Take time to check gauge.

STITCH GLOSSARY
lp(s) loop(s)
ch chain
CABLE CAST-ON
Cast on 2 sts. *Insert RH needle between the 2 sts on LH needle. Wrap yarn around RH needle as if to knit and pull yarn through to make a new st. Place new st on LH needle. Rep from * always inserting RH needle in between the last 2 sts on LH needle and until required number of sts is achieved.

PATTERN STITCH (over an even number of sts)
Row 1 (RS) Sl 1, k to end.
Row 2 Rep row 1.
Rows 3 and 4 Sl 1, *k1, p1; rep from *, end k1.
Rep rows 1–4 for pat st.

SHAWL
With crochet hook and waste yarn, ch 143. Cut yarn and draw end though lp on hook. Turn ch so bottom lps are at top and cut end is at LH side. With circular needles, beg 2 lps from opposite end, pick up and k 1 st in each of next 136 lps. Do not join. Work back and forth in pat st until piece measures approx 71"/180.5cm from beg (121 pat reps), end with a WS row. Rep rows 1 and 2.

YOU'LL NEED:
YARN (4)
39¼oz/1120g or 2030yd/1870m of any worsted weight wool blend
NEEDLES
Size 8 (5mm) circular needle, 24"/60cm long *or size to obtain gauge*
ADDITIONAL MATERIALS
Size H/8 (5mm) crochet hook
Contrasting worsted weight yarn (waste yarn)

FRINGE
Beg with first st on LH needle, *bind off 1 st, place st back on LH needle, then cable cast-on 19 sts (20 sts on needle). Knit 1 row. Purl 1 row. Bind off 21 sts knitwise. Rep from * across; bind off last st. To add fringe to opposite end, work as foll: with RS facing, release cut end from lp of waste yarn ch. Pull out 1 ch at a time, placing each st on LH needle. Rep rows 1 and 2 of pat st. Work fringe from ** to ** as for first end.

FINISHING
Block piece to measurements.

WAVE PATTERN Shawl

Jack Deutsch

YOU'LL NEED:

YARN
7oz/200g or 500yd/450m of any worsted weight wool blend

NEEDLES
One pair size 10 (6mm) needles *or size to obtain gauge*

FINISHED MEASUREMENTS
Approx 14½"/37cm wide x 65"/165cm long.

GAUGE
17 sts and 22 rows = 4"/10cm over wave pat using size 10 (6mm) needles.
Take time to check gauge.

STITCH GLOSSARY
WAVE PATTERN (multiple of 20 sts plus 2)
Row 1 (RS) P1, *p1, yo, k5, ssk, k4, k2tog, k5, yo, p1; rep from *, end p1.
Row 2 K1, *k1, p1, yo, p5, p2tog, p2, p2tog tbl, p5, yo, p1, k1; rep from *, end k1.
Row 3 P1, *p1, k2, yo, k5, ssk, k2tog, k5, yo, k2, p1; rep from*, end p1.
Row 4 K1, *k1, p3, yo, p1, p2tog, p6, p2tog tbl, p1, yo, p3, k1; rep from*, end k1.
Rep rows 1–4 for wave pat.

NOTE
Shawl can be worked from text or chart.

SHAWL
Cast on 62 sts. Knit next row. Work in wave pat until piece measures approx 65"/165cm from beg, end with a row 3. Knit next row. Bind off all sts loosely knitwise.

FINISHING
Block piece lightly to measurements.

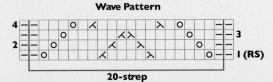

Wave Pattern

20-strep

StitchKey

☐ **K on RS, P on WS**

— **P on RS, K on WS**

○ **Yo**

⟋ **K2tog on RS, p2tog on WS**

⟍ **SSK on RS, p2tog-tbl on WS**

17

BEADED Leaf Lace

YOU'LL NEED:

YARN ❶
4oz/120g or 1650yd/1510m of any fingering weight wool

NEEDLES
Size 5 (3.75mm) circular needle, 24"/60cm long *or size to obtain gauge*
One size 6 (4mm) needle (for I-cord bind-off)

ADDITIONAL MATERIALS
Steel crochet hook size 12 (1mm)
900 size 6/0 silver-lined gold glass beads
Stitch markers

FINISHED MEASUREMENTS
Width across top edge Approx 86"/218.5cm.
Length from neck to point Approx 43"/109cm.

GAUGE
16 sts and 25 rows = 4"/10cm over chart pat 2 using size 5 (3.75mm) needles.
Take time to check gauge.

NOTES
1 The shawl is made from the top down and is composed of two identical sections that form a mirror image.
2 Only RS rows are shown on charts.
3 Chart 1, row 1, will inc 1 st per section (2 sts in total). Chart 1, row 27, and chart 2, row 23, will inc 4 sts per section (8 sts in total). All other charted rows will inc by 2 sts per section (4 sts in total).

STITCH GLOSSARY
ADD BEAD
Slide bead onto crochet hook. With hook in front, slip next st from LH needle onto hook. Slide bead onto st, then place st back on LH needle and knit.

SHAWL
With circular needle, cast on 6 sts. Knit next row.

BEG CHART 1
Row 1 (RS) K2, pm, work row 1 of chart 1 once, place marker (pm) for center of shawl, work row 1 of chart 1 once more—8 sts.
Row 2 and all WS rows K2, p to marker, sl marker, k2.
Row 3 K2, sl marker, work row 3 of chart 1 twice—12 sts.
Row 4 Rep row 2. Keeping 2 sts at beg of every RS row in garter st (k every row), cont to foll chart in this manner through row 27—64 sts.
Row 28 Rep row 2.

BEG CHART 2
First 24-row rep
Row 1 (RS) K2, slip marker, work row 1 of chart 2 twice—68 sts.
Row 2 and all WS rows K2, p to last 2 sts, end k2. Keeping 2 sts at beg of every RS row in garter st, cont to foll chart in this manner through row 23—116 sts.
Row 24 Rep row 2.
Second 24-row rep
Row 1 (RS) K2, slip marker, [work row 1 of chart 2 to first rep line, work 26-st rep twice, then work to end of chart row 1] twice—120 sts.
Row 2 and all WS rows K2, p to last 2 sts, end k2. Keeping 2 sts at beg of every RS row in garter st, cont to foll chart in this manner to row 23—168 sts.
Row 24 Rep row 2.
Third 24-row rep
Row 1 (RS) K2, slip marker, [work row 1 of chart 2 to first rep line, work 26-st rep 3 times, then work to end of chart row 1] twice—172 sts.
Row 2 and all WS rows K2, p to last 2 sts, end k2. Keeping 2 sts at beg of every RS row in garter st, cont to foll chart in this manner to row 23—220 sts.

Jack Deutsch

Row 24 Rep row 2.
Fourth 24-row rep
Row 1 (RS) K2, slip marker, [work row 1 of chart 2 to first rep line, work 26-st rep 4 times, then work to end of chart row 1] twice—224 sts.
Row 2 and all WS rows K2, p to last 2 sts, end k2. Keeping 2 sts at beg of every RS row in garter st, cont to foll chart in this manner through row 23—272 sts.
Row 24 Rep row 2.
Fifth 24-row rep
Row 1 (RS) K2, slip marker, [work row 1 of chart 2 to first rep line, work 26-st rep 5 times, then work to end of chart row 1] twice—276 sts.
Row 2 and all WS rows K2, p to last 2 sts, end k2. Keeping 2 sts at beg of every RS row in garter st, cont to foll chart in this manner through row 23—324 sts.
Row 24 Rep row 2.

Sixth 24-row rep

Row 1 (RS) K2, slip marker, [work row 1 of chart 2 to first rep line, work 26-st rep 6 times, then work to end of chart row 1] twice—328 sts.

Row 2 and all WS rows K2, p to last 2 sts, end k2. Keeping 2 sts at beg of every RS row in garter st, cont to foll chart in this manner through row 23—376 sts.

Row 24 Rep row 2.

Seventh 24-row rep

Row 1 (RS) K2, slip marker, [work row 1 of chart 2 to first rep line, work 26-st rep 7 times, then work to end of chart row 1] twice—380 sts.

Row 2 and all WS rows K2, p to last 2 sts, end k2. Keeping 2 sts at beg of every RS row in garter st, cont to foll chart in this manner through row 23—428 sts.

Row 24 Rep row 2.

Eighth 24-row rep

Row 1 (RS) K2, slip marker, [work row 1 of chart 2 to first rep line, work 26-st rep 8 times, then work to end of chart row 1] twice—432 sts.

Row 2 and all WS rows K2, p to last 2 sts, end k2. Keeping 2 sts at beg of every RS row in garter st, cont to foll chart in this manner through row 23—480 sts.

Row 24 Rep row 2.

BEG CHART 3

Row 1 (RS) K2, slip marker, [work row 1 of chart 3 to first rep line, work 26-st rep 9 times, then work to end of chart row 1] twice—484 sts.

Row 2 and all WS rows K2, p to last 2 sts, end k2. Keeping 2 sts at beg of every RS row in garter st, cont to foll chart in this manner through row 21—524 sts.

Row 22 Rep row 2.

I-Cord bind-off

With RS facing and straight needle, *k1, ssk, slip 2 sts on RH needle back to LH needle; rep from * until 2 sts rem, end ssk, fasten off last st.

FINISHING

Block piece to measurements.

Chart 3

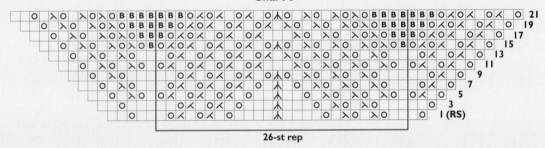

26-st rep

Chart 2

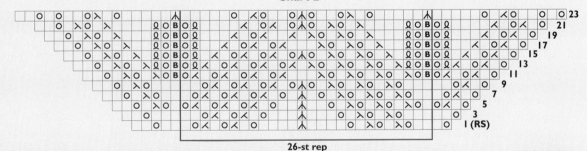

26-st rep

Chart 1

Stitch Key

☐	**K1**
○	**Yo**
⟋	**K2tog**
⟍	**SSK**
ℚ	**K1-tbl**
B	**Add bead**
人	**SK2P**
人	**S2KP2**

STAINED Glass

FINISHED MEASUREMENTS

Approx 72"/183cm wide x 25"/63.5cm long excluding fringe.

GAUGE

14¼ sts and 25½ rows = 4"/10cm over garter st using size 10 (6mm) needles. *Take time to check gauge.*

STRIP 1

With A, cast on 13 sts.
Rows 1–22 K1 tbl, k to last st, sl last st purlwise. Change to B.
Rows 23–44 Rep row 1. Change to MC.
Rows 45–66 Rep row 1. Change to C.
Rows 67–88 Rep row 1. Change to D.
Rows 89–110 Rep row 1. Change to MC.
Rows 111–132 Rep row 1. Change to E.
Rows 133–154 Rep row 1. Bind off.

STRIP 2

With MC, cast on 13 sts.
Joining
Row 1 (RS) K 1 tbl, k to last st, sl last st, insert LH needle into first st of row 1 of strip 1, sl st on RH needle onto LH needle and k the 2 sts tog.
Row 2 With MC, k 1 tbl, k to last st, sl last st purlwise.
Row 3 K1 tbl, k to last st, sl last st, insert LH needle into first st of row 3 of strip 1, sl st on RH needle onto LH needle and k the 2 sts tog.
Row 4 Rep row 2.
Row 5 K1 tbl, k to last st, sl last st, insert LH needle into first st of row 5 of strip 1, sl st on RH needle onto LH needle and k the 2 sts tog.
Row 6 Rep row 2.
Cont in this manner, joining strip 2 to strip 1 every RS row until 154 rows of MC have been completed and strips are joined.
Bind off.

STRIP 3

With F, cast on 13 sts.
Joining
Row 1 (RS) K1 tbl, k to last st, sl last st, insert LH needle into first st of row 1 of strip 2, sl st on RH needle onto LH needle and k the 2 sts tog.
Row 2 K1 tbl, k to last st, sl last st purlwise.
Row 3 K1 tbl, k to last st, sl last st, insert LH needle into first st of row 3 of strip 2, sl st on RH needle onto LH needle and k the 2 sts tog.
Row 4 Rep row 2.
Row 5 K1 tbl, k to last st, sl last st, insert LH needle into first st of row 5 of strip 2, sl st on RH needle onto LH needle and k the 2 sts tog.
Row 6 Rep row 2.
Cont in this manner, joining strip 3 to strip 2 every RS row until 22 rows of F have been completed. Refer to color placement diagram and cont to work color block pat and joining strips tog as established.

STRIPS 4–21

Refer to color placement diagram and cont to work and join strips tog, working 22 rows for each of the 7-block strips and 154 rows for each MC strip.

EDGING

With RS facing and crochet hook, join MC with a sl st in top right corner.
Rnd 1 (RS) Ch 1, sc in same place as joining, making sure that work lies flat, sc evenly around entire edge, working 3 sc

E		J	F		I	J		B	A		K	H		J	B		C	B		D
MC		MC	MC		MC	MC		MC	MC		MC	MC		MC	MC		MC	MC		MC
D		I	C		D	E		C	F		J	E		A	G		F	L		E
C	MC	H	K	MC	B	L	MC	G	E	MC	H	B	MC	K	C	MC	I	H	MC	G
MC		MC	MC		MC	MC		MC	MC		MC	MC		MC	MC		MC	MC		MC
B		G	E		L	F		H	K		C	L		H	E		J	G		C
A		F	J		H	C		B	J		I	A		F	L		B	A		F

in each corner, join rnd with a sl st in first sc.

Rnd 2 Ch 1, sc in each st across top edge to opposite top corner, *ch 3, sk next 2 sts, sc in next 2 sts; rep from * around rem 3 sides, join rnd with a sl st in first st. Fasten off.

FRINGE

Cut 12"/30.5cm strands of MC. Using 4 strands for each fringe, attach a fringe in each ch-3 sp along edging. Trim ends evenly.

COLOR KEY

(MC) Black

(A) Lavender

(B) Hollyhock

(C) Olive

(D) Blue

(E) Gold

(F) Fuchsia

(G) Viola

(H) Light blue

(I) Orange

(J) Forest green

(K) Red

(L) Turquoise

DOUBLE DIAMOND Shawl

YOU'LL NEED:

YARN 🔳

8¾oz/250g or 690yd/630m of any DK weight wool blend in lavender (MC)
3½oz/100g or 280yd/250m in pale green (CC)

NEEDLES

One pair size 6 (4mm) needles *or size to obtain gauge*
Size 6 (4mm) circular needle, 24"/60cm long

ADDITIONAL MATERIALS

Size G/6 (4mm) crochet hook
Contrasting sport weight yarn (waste yarn)

FINISHED MEASUREMENTS

Approx 24"/61cm wide x 62"/157.5cm long.

GAUGE

18 sts and 26 rows = 4"/10cm over St st using size 6 (4mm) needles.
Take time to check gauge.

STITCH GLOSSARY

lp(s) loops
ch chain

NOTES

1 Only RS rows are shown on charts.
2 Purl all WS rows.

SHAWL

With crochet hook and waste yarn, ch 105. Cut yarn and draw end though lp on hook. Turn ch so bottom lps are at top and cut end is at LH side. With straight needles and MC, beg 2 lps from RH end of ch, pick up and k 1 st in each of next 98 lps.
Knit one row. Purl one row.

BEG CHART 1
Row 1 (RS) Beg with st 1 and work

through st 17, then rep sts 2–17 4 times, then work sts 18–34. Cont to foll chart in this manner through row 32, then rep rows 1–32 5 times more, then rows 1–22 once. Cont as foll:

Rows 1 and 2 With MC, purl.
Rows 3 and 4 With CC, knit.
Rows 5 and 6 With MC, knit.
Rows 7 and 8 With CC, knit.
Row 9 With MC, knit.
Rows 10–12 With MC, purl.

BEG CHART 2
Row 1 (RS) Beg with st 1 and work through st 23, rep sts 6–23 3 times, then work sts 24–44. Cont to foll chart in this manner through row 38. Change to CC

and rep rows 3–38. Cont as foll:
Next 3 rows Purl. Bind off all sts knitwise.

OPPOSITE SIDE
Release cut end from lp of waste yarn ch. Pull out 1 ch at a time, placing each st on LH needle ready for a WS row. Cont as foll:
Row 1 (WS) With MC, purl.
Rows 2 and 3 With CC, knit.
Rows 4 and 5 With MC, knit.
Rows 6 and 7 With CC, knit.
Row 8 With MC, purl.
Rows 9–11 With MC, purl.

BEG CHART 2
Row 1 (RS) Beg with st 1 and work through st 23, rep sts 6–23 3 times, then

work sts 24–44. Cont to foll chart in this manner to row 38. Change to CC and rep rows 3–38. Cont as foll:
Next 3 rows Purl. Bind off all sts knitwise.

EDGING
With RS facing, circular needle and CC, pick up and k 256 sts evenly spaced across one long side edge. Knit next 4 rows. Bind off all sts loosely knitwise. Rep for opposite long side edge.

FINISHING
Block piece to measurements.

Chart 1

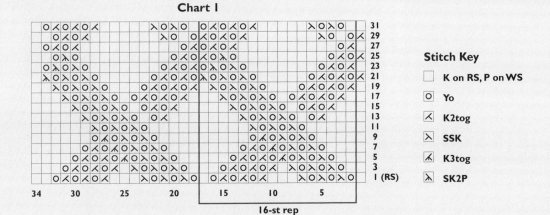

Stitch Key

☐	K on RS, P on WS
O	Yo
⟋	K2tog
⟍	SSK
⟋	K3tog
⟑	SK2P

34 30 25 20 15 10 5

31 29 27 25 23 21 19 17 15 13 11 9 7 5 3 1 (RS)

16-st rep

Chart 2

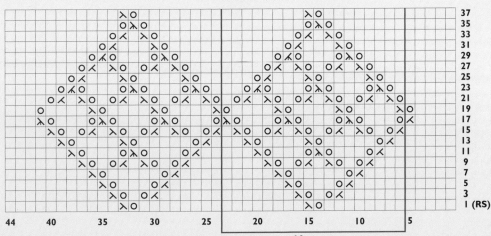

44 40 35 30 25 20 15 10 5

37 35 33 31 29 27 25 23 21 19 17 15 13 11 9 7 5 3 1 (RS)

AFGHAN Shawl

Jack Deutsch

FINISHED MEASUREMENTS
Approx 14"/35.5cm wide x 65"/165cm long excluding fringe.

GAUGE
9 sts and 6 rows = 4"/10cm over drop st pat using size 15 (10mm) needles.
Take time to check gauge.

STITCH GLOSSARY
DROP-STITCH PATTERN (multiple of 4 sts)
Row 1 (WS) Purl across wrapping yarn twice around needle for each st.
Row 2 *Sl next 4 sts to RH needle dropping extra wraps and forming 4 elongated sts, sl these 4 sts back to LH needle, working through all 4 sts at once, work [k4tog, p4tog] twice; rep from * to end.
Row 3 P2, purl across wrapping yarn twice around needle for each st, to the last 2 sts, end p2.
Row 4 K2, *sl next 4 sts to RH needle dropping extra wraps and forming 4 elongated sts, sl these 4 sts back to LH needle, working through all 4 sts at once, work [k4tog, p4tog] twice; rep from *, end k2.
Rep rows 1–4 for drop st pat.

SHAWL
Cast on 32 sts. Work in drop st pat until piece measures 65"/165cm from beg, end with a RS row. Bind off all sts purlwise.

FINISHING
Block piece to measurements.

FRINGE
Cut 42 stands 16"/40.5cm long. Using 3 strands for each fringe, attach 7 fringes evenly spaced across each end of shawl. Trim ends evenly.

DROP STITCH Shawl

Jack Deutsch

YOU'LL NEED:

YARN (4)
10½oz/300g or 680yd/620m of any worsted weight cotton

NEEDLES
Size 10 (6mm) circular needle, 40"/101cm long *or size to obtain gauge*

ADDITIONAL MATERIALS
Stitch markers

FINISHED MEASUREMENTS
Width across top edge Approx 72"/183cm.
Length from neck to bottom edge Approx 36"/91.5cm.

GAUGE
8¼ sts = 4"/10cm over drop st pat using size 10 (6mm) needles.
Take time to check gauge.

NOTES
1 Shawl is made in one piece from the top down.
2 Shawl is divided into four triangular sections that form the half-circle shape.

SHAWL
Cast on 4 sts.
Row 1 (inc) K into front and back of each st across—8 sts.

Row 2 [K2, pm] 3 times, k2. Markers indicate four sections: two side sections and two center sections.
Rows 3 and 4 Knit.
Row 5 (inc) K into front and back of each st across—16 sts.
Row 6 Knit.
Row 7 (inc) K into front and back of first st, k to last st, k into front and back of last st—18 sts.
Note From this point forward, each of the two side sections will have 1 more st than the two center sections.
Row 8 Knit.
Row 9 (inc) K1, *k1, yo, k2, yo, k1; rep from * to last st, end k1—26 sts (7 sts in each side panel and 6 sts in each center panel).
Row 10 Knit.
Row 11 K1, *k2, [k1, yo] twice, k2; rep from * to last st, end k1.
Row 12 Knit across, dropping extra wraps.
Row 13 (inc) K1, *k1, yo, k to 1 st before marker, yo, k1; rep from * to last st, end k1—34 sts.
Row 14 Knit.
Row 15 K1, [k2, *k1, yo twice; rep from * to 2 sts before marker, k2] 3 times, k2, rep from * to * to last 3 sts, end k3.
Row 16 Knit across, dropping extra wraps.
Rep rows 13–16 23 times more—218 sts (55 sts in each side panel and 54 sts in each center panel).
Row 109 Rep row 13—226 sts.
Rows 110–112 Knit.
Row 113 Rep row 13—234 sts.
Rows 114–116 Knit. Bind off last row loosely as foll: k first 2 sts. Sl these sts, one st at a time, back to LH needle, k these 2 sts tog, *k next st, sl 2 sts on RH needle, one st at a time, back to LH needle, k these 2 sts tog; rep from * until 1 st rem. Fasten off last st.

FINISHING
Block piece lightly to measurements.

SCALLOP-STITCH Wrap

YOU'LL NEED:

YARN
10½oz/300g or 750yd/690m of any
worsted weight wool

NEEDLES
Size 10 (6mm) needles *or size to
obtain gauge*
Two size 10 (6mm) dpns (for I-cord
edging)

FINISHED MEASUREMENTS
Approx 15½"/39cm wide x 65"/165cm
long excluding edging.

GAUGE
15 sts and 22 rows = 4"/10cm over
diamond scallop st.
Take time to check gauge.

STITCH GLOSSARY
**DIAMOND SCALLOP STITCH (multiple of 8
sts plus 2)**
Rows 1 and 3 (WS) Purl.
Row 2 K1, *wyib, insert RH needle under
running thread between st just worked
and next st and place on needle, k2, pass
running thread over the 2 knit sts, k2; rep
from *, end k1.
Row 4 K3, *wyib, insert RH needle under
running thread between st just worked
and next st and place on needle, k2, pass
running thread over the 2 knit sts, k2; rep
from *, end last rep k1.
Rep rows 1–4 for diamond scallop st.

WRAP
With straight needles, cast on 58 sts.
Work in diamond scallop st until piece
measures 65"/165cm from beg, end with
a WS row. Bind off.

I-CORDS (make 2)
With dpn, cast on 4 sts. Work in I-cord as
foll:
*Next row (RS) With 2nd dpn, k4, do not
turn. Slide sts back to beg of needle to
work next row from RS; rep from * until
piece measures 41"/104cm from beg.

Jack Deutsch

Cut yarn, leaving a long tail. Thread tail
into tapestry needle, then weave needle
through sts; fasten off securely.

FINISHING
Block piece to measurements.

LOOPED EDGING
With RS facing, pin an I-cord to bound-
off edge, forming five 1½"/4cm diameter

loops that are spaced approx 1¾/4.5cm
apart and making sure the 3rd loop is
centered. Sew in place. Rep for cast-on
edge.

IVY League

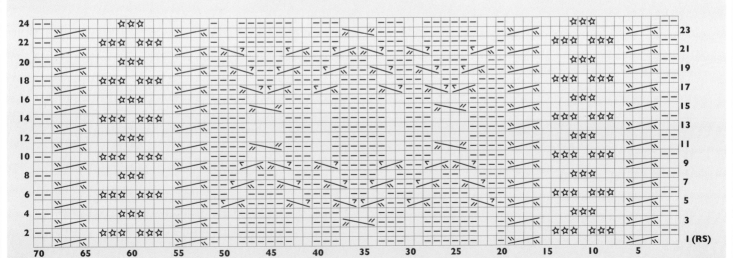

YOU'LL NEED:

YARN (5)
26¼oz/750g or 1290yd/1190m of any bulky weight wool

NEEDLES
One pair size 9 (5.5mm) needles *or size to obtain gauge*

ADDITIONAL MATERIALS
Cable needle
Size I/9 (5.5mm) crochet hook

FINISHED MEASUREMENTS
Approx 23½"/59.5cm wide x 55½"/141cm long excluding edging.

GAUGE
16 sts and 22 rows = 4"/10cm over St st. *Take time to check gauge.*

STITCH GLOSSARY
MS (make star) P3tog leaving sts on needle, yo, then p the same 3 sts tog again.
4-st RC Sl 2 sts to cn and hold in *back*, k2, k2 from cn.
4-st LC Sl 2 sts to cn and hold in *front*, k2, k2 from cn.
3-st RPC Sl next st to cn and hold in *back*, k2, p1 from cn.
3-st LPC Sl 2 sts to cn and hold in *front*, p1, k2 from cn.
ch chain

sc single crochet
sl st slip stitch

WRAP
Cast on 119 sts.
BEG CHART
Row 1 (RS) Beg with st 1 and work through st 68, then work sts 20–70. Cont to foll chart in this manner through row 24, then rep rows 1–24 11 times more. Bind off.

FINISHING
Block lightly to measurements.
EDGING
With RS facing and crochet hook, join yarn with a sl st in any corner.
Rnd 1 (RS) Ch 1, sc in same place as joining, making sure that work lies flat, work 3 sc evenly spaced, *ch 3, sl st in 3rd ch from hook (picot made), *work 4 sc evenly spaced, make picot; rep from * around, join rnd with a sl st in first sc. Fasten off.

Stitch Key
☐	K on RS, P on WS
⊟	P on RS, K on WS
⟋	3-st RPC
⟍	3-st LPC
⟋	4-st RC
⟍	4-st LC
☆☆☆	MS

TEXTURED ZIGZAG Shawl

Dan Howell

YOU'LL NEED:

YARN
Simply Soft, by Caron, 6oz/170g
skeins, each approx. 315yd/288m
(acrylic)
3 skeins #9712 Soft Blue

NEEDLES
One pair size 8 (5mm) needles *or size to obtain gauge*

FINISHED MEASUREMENTS
Approx 20½"/52cm wide x 63"/160cm
long excluding tassels.

GAUGE
15½ sts and 22¼ rows = 4"/10cm over
chart pat after blocking using size 8
(5mm) needles.
Take time to check gauge.

SHAWL
Cast on 79 sts loosely.
Next row (RS) Knit.
Next row K3, p73, k3.

BEG CHART
Row 1 (RS) Beg with st 1 and work
through st 25, rep sts 14–25 4 times, then
work sts 26–31. Cont to foll chart in this
manner through row 16, then rep rows
1–16 21 times more, end with a WS row.
Next row (RS) Knit.
Next row K3, p73, k3. Bind off all sts
knitwise.

FINISHING
Block piece to measurements.

TASSELS (make 14)
Leaving an 8"/20.5cm tail, cast on 7 sts
loosely. Knit 10 rows. Bind off 2 sts (tassel
top). Cut yarn, leaving a 10"/25.5cm tail,
then draw through st on RH needle to
fasten off. Remove rem 4 sts from LH
needle, then unravel them to form 6
loops. Thread long tail in tapestry needle.
Roll top of tassel tightly towards longer
tail. Use this tail to sew the side edge of
the roll to secure it in place, then
use same tail to wrap 4 times around
base of tassel top. Make a few sts to
secure wraps, then insert needle up
through center of tassel top so needle
exits center top. Remove needle. Trim
shorter tail even with bottom of loops.
Using longer tails to sew tassels to cast-
on and bound-off edges of shawl, sew
one to each corner, then one centered
beneath each St st zigzag.

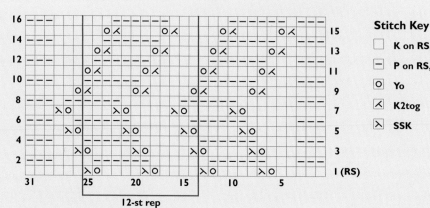

Stitch Key

☐	K on RS, P on WS
–	P on RS, K on WS
O	Yo
⟋	K2tog
⟍	SSK

12-st rep

SHORT-ROW Shawl

FINISHED MEASUREMENTS
Width across top edge
Approx 62"/157.5cm.
Length from neck to bottom edge
Approx 26"/66cm.

GAUGE
16 sts and 22 rows = 4"/10cm over St st
using size 10 (6mm) needles.
Take time to check gauge.

NOTES
1 Back section of shawl is worked vertically from side to side using short-row wrapping.
2 Each front section is worked out from the back section.

STITCH GLOSSARY
SHORT-ROW WRAPPING (wrap and turn—w&t)
1 On knit side, wyib, sl next st purlwise.
2 Move yarn between the needles to the front.
3 Sl the same st back to LH needle. Turn work, bring yarn to the purl side between the needles—one st wrapped.
4 When short rows are completed, work to just before the wrapped st. Insert RH needle under the wrap knitwise and knit it tog with next stitch on LH needle.

SHAWL
BACK SECTION
With crochet hook and waste yarn, ch 102. Cut yarn and draw end though lp on hook. Turn ch so bottom lps are at top and cut end is at LH side. With needles, beg 2 lps from opposite end, pick up and k 1 st in each of next 95 lps. Purl next row.

SHORT ROWS
Set-up row (WS) K5, p to last 5 sts, end k5.
Row 1 (RS) K 84, w&t.
Rows 2, 4, 6, 8 and 10 Purl to last 5 sts, end k5.
Row 3 K67, w&t.
Row 5 K50, w&t.
Row 7 K33, w&t.
Row 9 K16, w&t.
Row 11 Knit across, picking up wraps and knitting them tog with next st.
Rows 13, 15, 17 and 19 Knit.
Rows 12, 14, 16, 18 and 20 K5, p to last 5 sts, end k5.
Rep rows 1–20 9 times more, then rep rows 1–12 once more.

RIGHT FRONT SECTION
Dec row 1 (RS) K5, ssk, k to end.
Next row K5, p to last 5 sts, end k5. Rep last 2 rows 29 times more—65 sts.
Dec row 2 (RS) K5, ssk, k to end.
Dec row 3 K5, p to last 7 sts, end p2tog, k5.
Rep last 2 rows 26 times more, then dec row 1 once more—10 sts.
Work even in garter st (k every row) on all sts for 1"/2.5cm. Bind off.

Jack Deutsch

LEFT FRONT SECTION
With RS facing, release cut end from lp of waste yarn ch. Pulling out 1 ch at a time, place sts from back section on LH needle ready for a RS row.
Dec row 1 (RS) K to last 7 sts, end k2tog, k5.
Next row K5, p to last 5 sts, end k5. Rep last 2 rows 29 times more—65 sts.
Dec row 2 (RS) K to last 7 sts, end k2tog, k5.
Dec row 3 K5, p2tog tbl, p to last 5 sts, end k5.
Rep last 2 rows 26 times more, then dec row 1 once more—10 sts.
Work even in garter st on all sts for 1"/2.5cm. Bind off.

FINISHING
Block piece to measurements.

GLITTER and Gold

YOU'LL NEED:

YARN
5⅓oz/150g or 570yd/530m of any
worsted weight metallic
gold yarn (MC)
1¾oz/50g or 144yd/133m of any DK
weight wool blend in
dark brown (CC)

NEEDLES
Size 10 (6mm) circular needle,
24"/60cm long *or size to obtain gauge*

ADDITIONAL MATERIALS
Size F/5 (3.75mm) crochet hook

FINISHED MEASUREMENTS
Width across top edge Approx 46"/117cm.
Length from top edge to point Approx
26"/66cm.

GAUGE
12½ sts and 22 rows = 4"/10cm over
garter st using size 10 (6mm) needles.
Take time to check gauge.

STITCH GLOSSARY
ch chain
sc single crochet
sl st slip stitch

SHAWL
With MC, cast on 2 sts.
Row 1 (RS) K1, M1, k1—3 sts.
Row 2 K1, M1, k2—4 sts.
Row 3 K1, M1, k3—5 sts.
Row 4 K1, M1, k to end—6 sts.
Rep row 4 until there are 145 sts on
needle. Bind off all sts loosely knitwise.

EDGING
With RS facing and crochet hook, join
CC with a sl st in first bound-off st of top
edge.
Rnd 1 (RS) Ch 1, sc in same st a joining,
cont to sc in each bound-off st across,
turn to side edge; making sure that work
lies flat work: *ch 3, sc in side edge*;
rep from * to * 57 times more to before
bottom point, work (sc, ch 1, sc) in point,

ch 3, then rep from * to * 58 times to
before top edge, ch 3, join rnd with a sl st
in first sc.
Rnd 2 Ch 1, sc in same st as joining, *ch
2, skip next 2 sts, sc in next st; rep from *
across top edge, turn to side edge, work
5 dc in next ch-3 sp, **ch 1, skip next ch-3
sp, work 5 dc in next ch-3 sp**; rep from
** to ** to bottom ch-1 sp, work 5 dc in
ch-1 sp, work 5 dc in next ch-3 sp; rep
from ** to ** to top edge, join rnd with a
sl st in first sc. Fasten off.

Jack Deutsch

TANGO Shawl

YOU'LL NEED:

YARN
15½oz/440g (19¾oz/560g) or
1100yd/1010m (1400yd/1280m) of
any worsted weight nylon blend

NEEDLES
Size 8 (5mm) circular needle,
24"/60cm long *or size to obtain gauge*

SIZES
Instructions are written for
Small/Medium. Changes for
Large/X-Large are in parentheses.

FINISHED MEASUREMENTS
Width Approx 54 (62)"/127 (157.5)cm.
Length Approx 27 (29)"/68.5 (73.5)cm.

GAUGE
24 sts to 5"/12.5cm and 26 rows =
4"/10cm over pat st using size 8 (5mm)
needles.
Take time to check gauge.

STITCH GLOSSARY
PATTERN STITCH (multiple of 7 sts plus 2)
Row 1 (RS) K2, *k2tog, yo, k1, yo, ssk, k2;
rep from * to end.
Row 2 K2, *p5, k2; rep from * to end.
Rep rows 1 and 2 for pat st.

SHAWL
Beg at bottom edge, cast on 261 (296)
sts. Do not join. Work back and forth in
pat st until piece measures 14 (15)"/35.5
(38)cm from beg, end with a WS row.

DIVIDE FOR ARMHOLES
Next row (RS) Work across first 92 (106)
sts, join a second ball of yarn and work
across center 77 (84) sts, join a third ball
of yarn and work across last 92 (106) sts.
Working each section separately, work
even until armhole measures 8 (9)"/20.5
(23)cm, end with a WS row.
Next (joining) row (RS) With first ball of
yarn, work across all sts dropping second
and third balls—261 (296) sts. Cont
to work even until piece measures 27
(29)"/68.5 (73.5)cm from beg, end with a
WS row. Bind off all sts loosely.

FINISHING
Block piece to measurements.

Jack Deutsch

LEAF Shawl

Jack Deutsch

FINISHED MEASUREMENTS
Approx 18"/45.5cm wide x 68"/172.5cm long.

GAUGE
21 sts and 32 rows = 4"/10cm over wave and leaf pat st using size 5 (3.75mm) needles.
Take time to check gauge.

NOTE
1 Shawl is made in 2 halves, then joined tog using three-needle bind-off.
2 Shawl can be worked using text below or chart

STITCH GLOSSARY
WAVE AND LEAF PATTERN STITCH (multiple of 10 sts plus 5)
Row 1 (RS) K2, *yo, ssk, k8; rep from * to last 3 sts, end yo, ssk, k1.
Row 2 P3, *yo, p2tog, p5, p2tog tbl, yo, p1; rep from * to last 2 sts, end p2.
Row 3 K2, *k2, yo, ssk, k3, k2tog, yo, k1; rep from * to last 3 sts, end k3.
Row 4 P3, *p2, yo, p2tog, p1, p2tog tbl, yo, p3; rep from * to last 2 sts, end p2.
Row 5 K2, *k4, yo, SK2P, yo, k3; rep from * to last 3 sts, end k3.
Row 6 Purl.
Row 7 K2, k2tog, *yo twice, ssk, k3, k2tog, yo twice, SK2P; rep from * to last 4 sts, end yo twice, ssk, k2.
Row 8 P3, *work (p1, k1) in the 2 yo's, p5, work (k1, p1) in the 2 yo's, p1; rep from * to last 2 sts, end p2.
Row 9 K2, *k2, yo twice, SK2P, k1, k3tog, yo twice, k1; rep from * to last 3 sts, end k3.
Row 10 P3, *p1, work (p1, k1) in the 2 yo's, p3, work (k1, p1) in

the 2 yo's, p2; rep from * to last 2 sts, end p2.
Row 11 K2, *k3, yo twice, (sl 2, k3tog, p2sso)—S2K3P2 made, yo twice, k2; rep from * to last 3 sts, end k3.
Row 12 P3, *p2, work (k1, p1) in the 2 yo's, p1, work (p1, k1) in the 2 yo's, p3; rep from * to last 2 sts, end p2.
Row 13 K2, *k1, k3tog, yo twice, k3, yo twice, SK2P; rep from * to last 3 sts, end k3.
Row 14 P3, *p1, work (k1, p1) in the 2 yo's, p3, work (p1, k1) in the 2 yo's, p2; rep from * to last 2 sts, end p2.
Row 15 K2, k3tog, *yo twice, K5, yo twice, S2K3P2; rep from * to last 5 sts, end yo twice, SK2P, k2.
Row 16 P3, *work (k1, p1) in the 2 yo's, p5, work (p1, k1) in the 2 yo's, p1; rep from * to last 2 sts, end p2.
Row 17 K2, *k5, yo, ssk, k3; rep from * to last 3 sts, end k3.
Row 18 P3, *p2, p2tog tbl, yo, p1, yo, p2tog, p3; rep from * to last 2 sts, end p2.
Row 19 K2, *k2, k2tog, yo, k3, yo, ssk, k1; rep from * to last 3 sts, end k3.
Row 20 P3, *p2tog tbl, yo, p5, yo, p2tog, p1; rep from * to last 2 sts, end p2.
Row 21 K2, k2tog, *yo, k7, yo, SK2P; rep from * to last 4 sts, end ssk, k2.
Row 22 Purl.
Row 23 K2, *k2, k2tog, yo twice, SK2P, yo twice, ssk, k1; rep from * to last 3 sts, end k3.
Row 24 Rep row 12.
Row 25 K2, *k1, k3tog, yo twice, k3, yo twice, SK2P; rep from * to last 3 sts, end k3.
Row 26 Rep row 14.

Row 27 K2, k3tog, *yo twice, k5, yo twice, S2K3P2, p2sso; rep from * to last 5 sts, end yo twice, SK2P, k2.
Row 28 Rep row 8.
Row 29 K2, *k2, yo twice, SK2P, k1, k3tog, yo twice, k1; rep from * to last 3 sts, end k3.
Row 30 Rep row 10.
Row 31 K2, *k3, yo twice, S2K3P2, yo twice, k2; rep from * to last 3 sts, end k3.
Row 32 P3, *p2, work (p1, k1) in the 2 yo's, p1, work (k1, p1) in the 2 yo's, p3; rep from * to last 2 sts, end p2.
Rep rows 1–32 for wave and leaf pat st.

SHAWL
FIRST HALF
With circular needle. cast on 95 sts. Do not join. Working back and forth, knit 3 rows.
Next row (RS) K5, pm, work row 1 of wave and leaf pat st over center 85 sts, pm, k5.
Next row K5, sl marker, work row 2 of wave and leaf pat st over center 85 sts, sl marker, k5. Keeping 5 sts each side in garter st, cont to work as foll: work rows 3–6 once, rows 1–6 once, rows 1–32 seven times, then rows 1–27 once, end WS.
Piece measures approx 33"/84cm from beg. Leave sts on needle.

SECOND HALF
Work as for first half.

FINISHING
Block pieces lightly to measurements.

JOINING
With RS tog, hold shawl halves on two parallel circular needles. Insert straight needle knitwise into first st of each needle and wrap yarn around each needle as if to knit. Knit these 2 sts tog and sl them off the needles. *K the next 2 sts tog in the same manner. Sl first st on straight needle over the 2nd st and off the needle. Rep from * across row until all sts are bound off.

Wave and Leaf Pattern

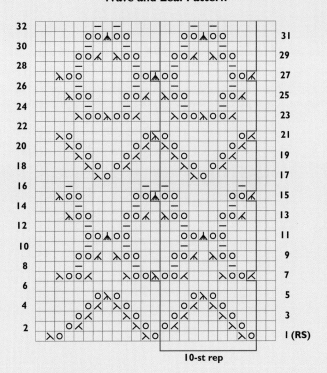

10-st rep

Stitch Key

☐	**K on RS, P on WS**
⊟	**P on RS, K on WS**
O	**Yo**
↘	**SSK on RS, p2tog-tbl on WS**
↙	**K2tog on RS, p2tog on WS**
⅄	**SK2P - Sl1, k2tog, psso**
⋏	**K3tog on RS, p3tog on WS**
⋔	**S2K3P2 - Sl2tog knitwise, k3tog, p2sso**

SNOWFLAKE Shawl

Jack Deutsch

YOU'LL NEED:

YARN

4oz/113g or 1250yd/1143m of any lace weight wool blend

NEEDLES

Two pairs size 4 (3.5mm) needles *or size to obtain gauge*

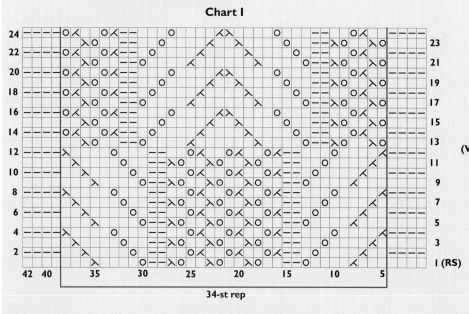

FINISHED MEASUREMENTS

Approx 19"/48cm wide x 76"/193cm long.

GAUGE

23 sts and 27 rows = 4"/10cm over chart pats after blocking using size 4 (3.5mm) needles.
Take time to check gauge.

NOTE

Shawl is made in 2 panels, then grafted tog.

SHAWL

PANEL 1

Cast on 110 sts loosely.

Beg chart 1

Row 1 (RS) Beg with st 1 and work through st 38, rep sts 5–38 twice, then work sts 39–42—110 sts. Cont to foll chart in this manner through row 24, then rep rows 1–24 3 times more, then rows 1–12 once. Cont as foll:

Row 1 (RS) Knit.

Row 2 K4, p to last 4 sts, end k4.

Row 3 K4, *yo, k2tog; rep from * to last 4 sts, end k4.

Row 4 K4, p to last 4 sts, end k4.

Row 5 K4, *k2tog, yo; rep from * to last 6 sts, end k2tog, k4—109 sts.

Row 6 K4, p to last 4 sts, end k4.

Piece should measure approx 17"/43cm from beg. Leave sts on needle. Cut yarn, leaving a 2yd/2m tail for grafting.

PANEL 2

Work chart 1 as for panel 1, then

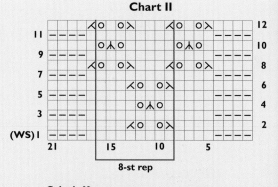

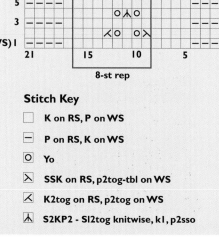

row rows 1–6.
Row 7 Knit.
Beg chart 2
Row 1 (WS) Beg with st 1 and work to st 16, rep sts 9–16 11 times, then work sts 17–21—109 sts. Cont to foll chart in this manner through row 12, then rep rows 1–12 until piece measures 59"/150cm from beg, end with a WS row. Knit next row. Leave sts on needle.

JOINING PANELS
Graft the 2 panels tog using Kitchener stitch. Place panel 1 in front of panel 2, WS facing and needle tips pointing to the right. Thread tail in tapestry needle. Insert tapestry needle into first st on front needle as if to purl, then pull yarn through, leaving st on needle. Insert the needle into the first stitch on the back needle as if to knit, then pull yarn through, leaving st on needle. Cont as foll:
Step 1 Insert needle into first st on front needle as if to knit and slip it off needle.
Step 2 Insert needle into next st on front needle as if to purl, then pull yarn through leaving st on needle.
Step 3 Insert needle into first st on back needle as if to purl and slip it off needle.
Step 4 Insert needle into next st on back needle as if to knit, then pull yarn through leaving st on needle. Taking care to maintain gauge, rep steps 1–4 until you have grafted all sts, rep steps 1 and 2 for the garter st borders.

FINISHING
Block piece to measurements.

Jack Deutsch

YOU'LL NEED:

YARN (4)
22oz/630g or 800yd/730m of any worsted weight mohair blend

NEEDLES
One pair size 11 (8mm) needles *or size to obtain gauge*

FINISHED MEASUREMENTS
Width across top edge Approx 76"/193cm.
Length from neck to point Approx 35"/89cm.

GAUGE
11 sts and 19¾ rows = 4"/10cm over seed st using size 11 (8mm) needles.
Take time to check gauge.

NOTES
1 Shawl is made vertically from top corner to top corner.
2 Picot edging is added as you work by casting on and binding off sts.
3 Use knit-on method for casting on.

STITCH GLOSSARY
SEED STITCH (over an even number of sts)
Row 1 *K 1, p 1; rep from * to end.
Row 2 Knit the p sts and purl the k sts

SHAWL
FIRST HALF
Note To inc 1 st in seed st, p into front and back of st if st is to be purled, or k into front and back of st if st is to be knitted.
Cast on 2 sts.
Row 1 (WS) K1, p1.
Row 2 (RS) Cast-on 3 sts, bind off 3 sts, k1.
Row 3 K1, inc 1 st in next st.
Row 4 Cast-on 3 sts, bind off 3 sts, work in seed st to end.
Row 5 Work in seed st to last st, inc 1 st in last st.
Rep rows 4 and 5 until there are 95 sts on needle (not including 3 cast-on sts), end with a WS row. Piece should measure approx 38"/96.5cm from beg.

SECOND HALF
Note To dec 1 st in seed st, p2tog if next to last st is to be purled or k2tog if next to last st is to be knitted.
Next row (RS) Cast on 3 sts, bind off 3 sts, work in seed st to end.
Next row Work in seed st to last 2 sts, work next 2 sts tog.
Rep these 2 rows until 2 sts rem. Bind off in seed st.

FINISHING
Block piece lightly to measurements.

RUFFLED Capelet

YOU'LL NEED:

YARN ❸
8oz/226g or 660yd/610m of any DK weight variegated wool

NEEDLES
Size 5 (3.75mm) circular needle, 40"/100cm long *or size to obtain gauge*
Two size 5 (3.75mm) double-pointed needles (dpns) for I-cord tie

FINISHED MEASUREMENTS
Width across bottom edge Approx 45"/114.5cm.
Length from neck to bottom edge Approx 9"/23cm.

GAUGE
22 sts and 26 rows = 4"/10cm over St st using size 5 (3.75mm) needles.
Take time to check gauge.

NOTE
Ruffles are added after knitting is completed.

CAPELET
With circular needle, cast on 240 sts. *Do not join.*
Working back and forth, knit next 2 rows.
Inc row 1 (WS) K12, *knit in front and back of next st, k26; rep from * 7 times more, end M1, k11—249 sts. Cont as foll:
Next row (RS) Sl 1 wyif, k to end.
Next row Sl 1 wyif, k2, p to last 3 sts, end k3.
Rep last 2 rows until piece measures 3¾"/9.5cm from beg, end with a WS row.
Dec row 2 (RS) Sl 1 wyif, k8, *SK2P, k9; rep from * to last 12 sts, end SK2P, k9—209 sts.
Next row Sl 1 wyif, k2, p to last 3 sts, end k3.
Dec row 3 (RS) Sl 1 wyif, *k17, SK2P*; rep from * to * twice more, k87, **SK2P, k17**; rep from ** to ** twice more, end k1—197 sts.
Next row Knit—for center ruffle garter st ridge.

TUCK
Row 1 (RS) Sl 1 wyif, k to end.
Row 2 Sl 1 wyif, k2, p to last 3 sts, end k3. Rep these 2 rows twice more.
Next (tuck) row (RS) Sl first st knitwise onto RH needle, on WS, insert tip of RH needle in top of first p-st of 6 rows below, sl

both sts to LH needle, then k them both tog, *sl next st knitwise onto RH needle, on WS, insert tip of RH needle in top of next p-st of 6 rows below. Sl both sts to LH needle, then k them both tog; rep from * to end.
Next row Sl 1 wyif, k to end. Rep rows 1 and 2 once more.
Dec row 4 (RS) Sl 1 wyif, k15, *SK2P, k15; rep from * to end—177 sts.
Rep row 2 once, then rows 1 and 2 3 times.
Dec row 5 (RS) Sl 1 wyif, k14, *SK2P, k13; rep from *, end k1—157 sts.
Rep row 2 once, then rows 1 and 2 3 times.
Dec row 6 (RS) Sl 1 wyif, k13, *SK2P, k11; rep from *, end k2—137 sts.
Rep row 2 once, then rows 1 and 2 3 times.
Dec row 7 (RS) Sl 1 wyif, k12, *SK2P, k9; rep from *, end k3—117 sts.
Next row Knit—for top ruffle garter st ridge.

DRAWSTRING CASING
Rows 1 and 3 Knit.
Row 2 Purl.
Row 4 Knit for garter st turning ridge.
Rows 5 and 7 Knit.
Rows 6 and 8 Purl. Bind off.

BOTTOM RUFFLE
With RS facing and circular needle, skip first st, pick up and k 1 st in each of next 238 sts, leaving last st unworked.
Next row (WS) Knit.
Next (inc) row (RS) Knit in front and back of each st to end—476 sts.
Next row Knit.
Next (inc) row (RS) Knit in front and back of each st to end—952 sts.
Next row Knit. Bind off all sts knitwise.

CENTER RUFFLE
With RS facing, bottom edge at top and circular needle, skip first st of center ruffle garter st ridge, pick up and k 1 st in each of next 195 sts, leaving last st unworked.
Next row (WS) Knit.
Next (inc) row (RS) Knit in front, back and front of each st to end—585 sts.
Next row Knit.
Bind off all sts knitwise.

TOP RUFFLE
With RS facing, bottom edge at top and circular needle, skip

first st of top ruffle garter st ridge, pick up and k 1 st in each of next 115 sts, leaving last st unworked.

Next row (WS) Knit.

Next (inc) row (RS) Knit in front, back and front of each st to end—345 sts.

Next row Knit.

Bind off all sts knitwise.

FINISHING

Fold drawstring casing to WS along garter st turning ridge and sew in place.

DRAWSTRING

With dpns, cast on 3 sts. Work in I-cord as foll:

*__Next row (RS)__ With 2nd dpn, k3, do not turn. Slide sts back to beg of needle to work next row from RS; rep from * until piece measures 52"/132cm from beg.

Cut yarn leaving a long tail. Thread tail into tapestry needle, then weave needle through sts; fasten off securely. Thread drawstring through casing.

Jack Deutsch

DIAGONAL Drop-Stitch Shawl

Jack Deutsch

YOU'LL NEED:

YARN 4
19½oz/550g or 1080yd/990m of any worsted weight nylon blend

NEEDLES
One pair size 10 (6mm) needles *or size to obtain gauge*

ADDITIONAL MATERIALS
Cable needle
Size H/8 (5mm) crochet hook

FINISHED MEASUREMENTS
Approx 23 x 54"/58.5 x 137cm.

GAUGE
19 sts and 28 rows = 4"/10cm over St st using size 10 (6mm) needles.
Take time to check gauge.

STITCH GLOSSARY
6 RC Sl 3 sts to cn and hold to *back*, k3, k3 from cn.
LT Knit into the back of 2nd st on needle, leave on LH needle, k into 1st and 2nd sts together, drop off needle.
sc single crochet

SHAWL
Cast on 4 sts.

BEG CHART-INC SLANTED EDGE
Beg with row 1, work 38 rows of chart—40 sts. Cont in pat as established,

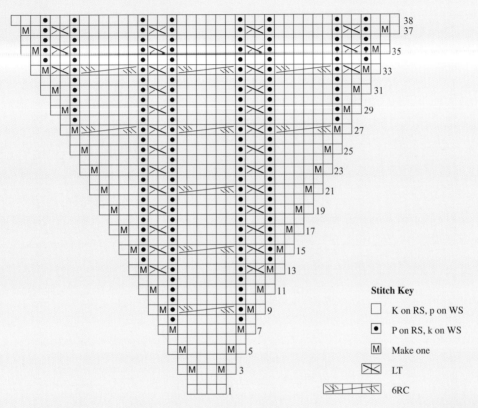

Stitch Key

☐ K on RS, p on WS

• P on RS, k on WS

M Make one

⧖ LT

⧗ 6RC

inc 1 st each side as established until 124 sts (60 inc's total each side), working inc sts in pat.

STRAIGHT SECTION

Note Read section before beg to knit. When a purl st is the 2nd to last st on a RS row, drop the st and k last st instead of k2tog at end.
Next row (RS) K1, M1, work in pat to last 2 sts, k2tog. Work 1 row even. Work last 2 rows until 14 LT cables have been worked.

DEC SLANTED EDGE

Note Read section before beg to knit. When a purl st is the 2nd st on needle on a RS row, k1, drop the p st instead of ssk; and when a purl st is the 2nd to the last st on RS row, drop the p st, k1 instead of k2tog.
Next row (RS) Ssk, work in pat to last 2 sts, k2tog. Work 1 row even. Work last 2 rows until 4 sts rem. Bind off, dropping any remaining p sts. Be sure that all p sts are completely unraveled.

FINISHING

Block pieces to measurements. Work 1 row of sc around entire edge of shawl.

LACY Shawl

YOU'LL NEED:

YARN
16oz/454g or 800yd/731m of any worsted weight variegated cotton

NEEDLES
One pair size 8 (5mm) knitting needles *or size to obtain gauge*

ADDITIONAL MATERIALS
Size I/9 (5.5mm) crochet hook
Stitch markers

FINISHED MEASUREMENTS
Approx 19½ x 48"/49.5 x 122cm.

GAUGE
17 sts and 20 rows = 4"/10cm over St st using size 8 (5mm) needles.
Take time to check gauge.

STITCH GLOSSARY
SK2P Sl 1 st knitwise, k2tog, psso.
Sssk Sl 3 sts knitwise one at a time to RH needle. Insert tip of LH needle into fronts of all 3 sts, and knit them together.
ch Chain
dc Double crochet
Dc2tog Double crochet 2 sts together.
Dc3tog Double crochet 3 sts together.
Tr Treble

NOTES
1 When working RS rows, read chart from right to left; when working WS rows, read chart from left to right.
2 Place markers between the different charted pattern sts to help keep your place.

SHAWL
Cast on 91 sts, and k 7 rows.

BEGIN CHART
Row 1 (RS) Beg with first st, work to beg of 37-st rep, work 37-st rep twice, work to end of row.
Cont to foll chart in this way until piece measures approx 42"/106.5cm (or desired length without crochet border), end with a WS row.
Note Crochet border adds approx 3"/7.6cm to each end.
Bind off.

CROCHET BORDER
With WS facing, rejoin yarn to bound-off edge of wrap, and work as foll across 91 bound-off sts:
Row 1 Ch 3 (counts as 1 dc), dc in next st, *ch 2, skip 2 sts, dc in each of the next 3 sts; rep from * end, dc in next 2 sts. Turn.
Row 2 Ch 2 and dc in next st (counts as dc2tog over first 2 sts), *ch 4, skip ch-2 sp, dc3tog over next 3 dc; rep from * to end, end dc2tog instead of dc3tog. Turn.
Row 3 Ch 7 (counts as 1 dc and 4 ch), *dc in next dc3tog, ch 4; rep from * to end, dc in last dc2tog.
Row 4 Ch 1, sc in first dc, *7 tr in next dc, sc in next dc; rep from * to end, working last sc in 3rd ch of ch 7. Fasten off.
Work along cast-on edge the same way.

FINISHING
Block piece flat to show lace patterns.

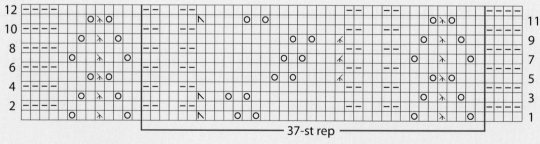

37-st rep

STITCH KEY
☐ k on RS, p on WS
⊟ p on RS, k on WS
⊙ yarn over
↗ SK2P
◣ sssk
◿ k3tog